D

796.06
PAN

Pancella, Peggy
Playground safety

C-1

$25.36
BC#34880000025762

DATE DUE	BORROWER'S NAME

796.06
PAN

BC#34880000025762 $25.36

Pancella, Peggy
Playground safety

C-1

Morrill E.S.
Chicago Public Schools
1431 North Leamington Avenue
Chicago, IL 60651

Be Safe!

Playground Safety

by Peggy Pancella

Heinemann Library
Chicago, Illinois

© 2005 Heinemann Library,
a division of Reed Elsevier Inc.
Chicago, Illinois

Customer Service 888-454-2279
Visit our website at www.heinemannlibrary.com

Designed by Heinemann Library
Page layout by Roslyn Broder
Printed and bound in China by South China Printing Co. Ltd.

09 08 07 06 05
10 9 8 7 6 5 4 3 2 1

Library of Congress Cataloging-in-Publication Data
Pancella, Peggy.
  Playground safety / Peggy Pancella.
     v. cm. -- (Be safe!)
  Includes bibliographical references and index.
  Contents: What is safety? -- Safe playgrounds -- Check the equipment -- Safety rules -- Playing with others -- Swings -- Slides -- Climbing equipment -- Seesaws -- Merry-go-rounds -- Other ways to play -- Strangers -- Playground accidents -- Safety tips.
  ISBN 1-4034-4934-1 (hardcover) -- ISBN 1-4034-4943-0 (pbk.)
  1. Playgrounds--Safety measures--Juvenile literature. [1. Playgrounds--Safety measures. 2. Safety.] I. Title.
  GV424.P36 2004
  796'.06'8--dc22
                                        2003024065

Acknowledgments
The author and publisher are grateful to the following for permission to reproduce copyright material:
Cover photograph by Warling Studios/Heinemann Library
p. 4 Will Hart/Photo Edit, Inc.; p. 5 Bill Aron/Photo Edit, Inc.; pp. 6, 7, 12, 17 Warling Studios/Heinemann Library; p. 8 Cathy Melloan Resources/Photo Edit, Inc.; p. 9 Graham Tim/Corbis Sygma; pp. 10, 15, 23, 28, 29 David Young-Wolff/Photo Edit, Inc.; p. 11 Tom Stewart/Corbis; p. 13 Mary Kate Denny/PhotoEdit, Inc.; p. 14 Michael Newman/Photo Edit, Inc.; p. 16 Jose Carillo/Photo Edit, Inc.; p. 18 Cassy Cohen/Photo Edit, Inc.; p.19 LWA-Dann Tardif/Corbis; pp. 20, 21 Michelle D. Bridwell/Photo Edit, Inc.; p. 22 Karl Weatherly/Corbis; p. 24 Terri Froelich/Index Stock; p. 25 Ariel Skelley/Corbis; p. 26 Greg Williams/Heinemann Library; p. 27 Rob Lewine/Corbis

Every effort has been made to contact copyright holders of any material reproduced in this book. Any omissions will be rectified in subsequent printings if notice is given to the publisher.

Contents

Some words are shown in bold, **like this.** You can find out what they mean by looking in the glossary.

What Is Safety?

It is important for everyone to stay safe. Being safe means keeping out of danger. It means staying away from things or people that could hurt you.

Safety is important in everything you do. One good place to be safe is at the playground. Playgrounds can be fun if you are careful. Learning some rules about playgrounds can help you stay safe.

Safe Playgrounds

Some ground **surfaces** are safer to land on than others are. Wood chips, sand, small pebbles, and rubber **shreds** or mats are softer surfaces. **Concrete, asphalt,** dirt, and grass are harder surfaces.

Safe playgrounds should also be clean.
Watch out for trash, and tell an adult if you
see dangerous things like broken glass. Pick
up after yourself to keep the playground
clean for others.

Check the Equipment

Before using playground **equipment,** check to be sure it is safe. Watch for parts that are rusty, sharp, or loose. Do not use equipment that looks broken or dangerous. Tell an adult about any problems you find.

Playground equipment is made to keep you safe from falls and other dangers. But do not treat equipment roughly or use it in wrong ways. You could break the equipment or hurt yourself.

Playing It Safe

Always have an adult watch you at the playground. Playing alone can sometimes be unsafe. Adults can watch for trouble and help you if you get hurt.

Playing at night or in bad weather is unsafe, too. Clothing can also be dangerous. Loose shoelaces may trip you. Laces and jacket strings can get caught in **equipment** and hurt you.

Playing with Others

It can be lots of fun to play with friends at the playground. Taking turns with the **equipment** can help you get along and keep you safe.

Sometimes children may push, fight, crowd others, or throw sand or dirt. If this happens, you can leave the area or ask an adult for help.

Swings

There are different kinds of swings, but they all need to be used safely. Always sit on swings instead of standing, and hold on with both hands.

When you are finished, stop the swing and get off slowly. Step away quickly and carefully so others on swings do not bump into you by **accident**.

Slides

When you slide, always use the ladder or steps to climb up. If you climb up the slide, someone sliding down could bump you. Do not push or crowd too close to the person in front of you.

Wait until the slide is clear before riding down. Sit on your bottom and slide down feet first. At the bottom, step aside to get out of the next person's way.

Climbing Equipment

Many playgrounds have lots of climbing **equipment**. Equipment comes in many different shapes and sizes. Some large kinds of equipment include slides, bridges, and poles.

Always use both hands when you are climbing. Watch for others who are using the equipment or standing below you. Stay off equipment that is wet or slippery.

Seesaws

Seesaws are for two people to use together. Riders sit at each end of a long board or pole. The seesaw is **balanced** in the middle so its ends move up and down.

Hold the handles of the seesaw and rock gently. Never sit backward or stand on a seesaw. When you finish, both riders should get off at the same time to keep the seesaw balanced.

Merry-go-rounds

Some playgrounds have merry-go-rounds that spin in circles. These can go fast or slow. Make sure the merry-go-round is completely stopped before getting on or off.

While you ride, keep your hands and feet in and hold on tight. If you feel dizzy, get off the merry-go-round. Sit quietly in a safe place until you feel better.

Other Ways to Play

Not all playgrounds have the same **equipment**. Some have different areas for younger and older children. To be safe, use only equipment that is meant for children your age.

Playgrounds sometimes have sandboxes and equipment that bounces or spins. Some have large open areas. You can run and fly kites there. Share the areas and equipment so you do not bump into others or get hurt.

Strangers

Sometimes you may see people you do not know at a playground. They are strangers to you. Some strangers are nice, but others could try to hurt you.

If a stranger tries to touch or talk to you, move away and tell a trusted adult. Never go anywhere with strangers. Do not take money or other gifts from them, either.

Playground Accidents

Even if you are careful, you can still get hurt at a playground. You might slip or fall, or someone might bump you by **accident.** If someone gets hurt, ask an adult to help.

An adult can clean small cuts or scrapes and put on bandages. If a person is badly hurt, do not try to move him or her. Stay nearby until help arrives.

Safety Tips

- Never play alone at a playground. Go with an adult or group of friends.

- Make sure that the playground is clean and the **equipment** is safe.

- Do not take chances or show off. Use the playground equipment properly.

- Take turns, share the equipment, and play fairly.

- If you have a problem, tell an adult you trust about it.

Glossary

accident something that happens unexpectedly

asphalt dark-colored substance used for paving streets and parking lots

balanced having equal weight on both sides

concrete hard material made by mixing cement, gravel, sand, and water

equipment supply or machine used for a certain activity

shred small strip or piece of something

surface top or outer layer of something

Index